Scythe and Seed
By Kenya T. Coviak

Eat something.

SCYTHE AND SEED: An Autumnal Cookbook
My Magical Cottage Core Life

Published by Spiral Moon Circle Publishing, 2024
Troy MI
ISBN 978-0-9914926-3-3

Recipe Locations

Hi there!

I wanted to start our fourth year with a tasty offering. I love recipe sharing. I hope you will like these.

I pray they bring you joy and sustenance. As always, don't be afraid to experiment.

This second cookbook contains recipes with a bit MORE in flavors, steps, and variety. We've come a long way together.

So, put this on the shelf with your Big Book of Stuff.

Let's get started.

I once did an episode on lovage. My lovage mini forest is huge and aggressively gorgeous. It comes back every year, since it's a perennial after all. I have so much, and during fall you can grab it up before it's gone and make this recipe.

Herb-Roasted Rabbit with Lovage and Rosehip Glaze

Ingredients you will need:

- 1 whole rabbit, cleaned and cut into pieces
- 2 tbsp fresh lovage, chopped or 1,tsp dried
- 2 tbsp olive oil
- Salt and pepper to taste
- 1/4 cup rosehip syrup
- 2 tbsp balsamic vinegar
- 2 tbsp ground spiceberry (optional)

Instructions:
Preheat the oven to 375°F (190°C).

In a small bowl, mix chopped lovage, olive oil, salt, and pepper. If you have it, add a bit of spiceberry.

Rub the herb mixture all over the rabbit pieces.

Place the rabbit in a roasting pan and roast for about 1 hour, or until the internal temperature reaches 160°F (71°C).

During the last 15 minutes of roasting, brush the rabbit with the rosehip glaze every several times.
2

While the rabbit is roasting, prepare the glaze by mixing rosehip syrup and balsamic vinegar in a small sauce pot or skillet. Simmer over low heat until slightly thickened, about 5 minutes.

Once done, let the rabbit rest for 10 minutes before serving.

Serve with roasted vegetables, crumbly bread, and drizzle with any of the remaining glaze.

We have a lot of rabbits around here. But all rabbits aren't safe for eating. So buy them from a farmer. Or even better, barter with an ethical hunter. Here in Detroit, you can get them at the grocery store, too.

Let's continue with our rabbit and lovage combo.

But first, let's talk about rose petals as an ingredient. Did you know you can add them to your sauces?

It's not just the hips that have flavor.

It's the same thing with rose jam. You can make your meal have more flavors by adding it to dishes. Just saying.

Rabbit Ragu with Lovage Pappardelle

Ingredients you will need:

For the ragu:
- 1 rabbit, deboned and meat cut into small pieces
- 1 onion, finely chopped
- 2 carrots, finely diced
- 2 celery stalks, finely diced
- 3 garlic cloves, minced
- 1 cup red wine
- 1 can (14 oz) crushed tomatoes
- 2 tbsp tomato paste
- 1 tsp dried oregano
- 2 bay leaves
- Salt and pepper to taste
- 2 tbsp olive oil

For the lovage pappardelle:
- 2 cups all-purpose flour
- 2 eggs
- 1/4 cup fresh lovage, finely chopped
- 1/2 tsp salt
- Water as needed

Instructions for the ragu:

4

Heat the olive oil in a large pot, or Dutch oven, over medium heat. Add rabbit pieces and brown on all sides, about 5-7 minutes.

Remove the rabbit and set aside. In the same pot, add onions, carrots, celery, and garlic. (You can change the flavor by substituting parsnips for carrots. It tastes a bit richer.)

Cook until softened, about 5 minutes.

Add wine and simmer until reduced by half, about 4 to 6 minutes.

Add the crushed tomatoes, tomato paste, oregano, bay leaves, salt, and pepper. Stir well.

Now you can return the rabbit to the pot.

Bring it all to a boil, then reduce heat to low. Cover and simmer for 2-3 hours, stirring occasionally, until the rabbit is very tender. A Dutch oven is great for this.

Remove the bay leaves and shred the rabbit meat with two forks.

Let's make the lovage pappardelle:
Mix the flour, chopped lovage, and salt on a clean surface. Make a well in the center.
Crack eggs into the well and gradually work the flour into eggs, using a fork, until it's all incorporated.

Knead your dough until it's smooth, adding water if needed.

Let it rest for 30 minutes.

Roll out your dough thinly and cut into wide strips for pappardelle.

Now, cook in boiling salted water for 2-3 minutes until al dente.

Toss cooked pappardelle with the rabbit ragu and serve it up hot.

Now listen, some people are gonna get weird about eating rabbit. But it's a common dish. Not only that, but in a pinch, it can feed a lot of people.

Trying new tastes is fun sometimes. Sharing new dishes and meats can be a group experience in the kitchen and dining room. Try it.

When I was younger, I was taught that if the meat is a bit gamey for your taste, there are remedies. You can soak the meat in buttermilk for a few hours first. You can marinate in vinegar. You can make a custom rub they already enjoy on other meats.

Don't be afraid. You may find a new favorite other white meat.

It's getting chilly outside, and meat is kinda a thing here in the Midwest. Turkeys are shaking their tail feathers off (surprise, Mom Joke). So, let's warm them up, in a nice hot oven.

Rosehip (or Gooseberry) and Turkey Meatballs
(my bushes threw a lot of hips this year, so the theme continues)

Ingredients you will need:

- 1 lb ground turkey
- 1/4 cup rosehip jam, (or gooseberry jam)
- 1/4 cup breadcrumbs
- 1 egg, beaten
- 1 small bunch of nodding onions, chopped
- 2 cloves garlic, minced
- 1 tsp dried thyme
- Salt and pepper to taste
- 2 tbsp cooking oil

For the sauce:
- 1/2 cup rosehip syrup, (or gooseberry syrup)
- 1/4 cup apple cider vinegar
- 1 tbsp soy sauce (or liquid aminos)
- 1 tsp cornstarch mixed with 1 tbsp water

Instructions:

Preheat your oven to 375°F (190°C).

(Trust me, cooking in a room temperature oven only leads to bad times and medical bills.)

In a large bowl, mix ground turkey, rosehip jam, breadcrumbs, egg, nodding onions, garlic, thyme, salt, and pepper until well combined.
7

Make small meatballs, about 1 inch in diameter.

Heat your cooking oil in an oven-safe skillet over medium heat. Brown the meatballs on all sides, about 5 minutes.

Transfer the skillet to the preheated oven and bake for 15-20 minutes, or until meatballs are cooked through (internal temperature of 165°F or 74°C).

While meatballs are baking, it's time to make the sauce:

 In a small saucepan, combine rosehip syrup, apple cider vinegar, and soy sauce (or liquid aminos). Then bring to a simmer over medium heat.

Add the cornstarch slurry and cook, stirring constantly, until the sauce thickens. Take your time and don't rush this. It will only take a couple of minutes. Rushing makes lumps.

Once the meatballs are done, pour the sauce over them and serve.

Now, these are great for potlucks because they are easy to transport in a slow cooker. You know Midwestern people LOVE slow cookers.

Now, this next one might not be to your taste. That's ok. But there are many more things in the world than burgers and nuggets. Nothing wrong with those. But some people like their food REAALLLLLY fresh. Like, "catch it in the trap" fresh.

My Grandma Earlene Horner used to have a semi pet raccoon when she was a child. She kept a jar of honey on the kitchen table for it. It would run in from outside for a dipped paw full of honey.

When I was dating my husband, she liked him. When he brought her a fresh raccoon for her table, I think matchmaking was solidified. He passed the Grandma test.

So here's a recipe for you to enjoy in honor of wise grandmothers who know a good match when they see one.

Slow-Cooked Raccoon with Root Vegetables

Ingredients you will need:

3-4 lbs raccoon meat, cleaned and cut into large pieces (store bought is just fine)
- 2 onions, quartered
- 3 carrots, cut into chunks
- 3 parsnips, cut into chunks
- 1 golden beet, cut into chunks
- 1 sweet potato, cut into large cubes
- 4 cloves garlic, minced
- 2 cups chicken, raccoon, or vegetable broth
- 1/4 cup apple cider vinegar, or magnolia leaf vinegar
- 2 tbsp tomato paste
- 1 tbsp dried orange thyme
- 2 bay leaves
- Salt and pepper to taste
- dried ramp flakes, if you have them

Instructions:

If using a raccoon from a hunter, make sure the meat is inspected and properly cleaned by a professional to ensure safety.

Preheat the oven to 300°F (150°C).

Season the raccoon pieces generously with salt and pepper. Add a bit of dried ramp flakes for that extra flavor, if you have it.

In a large Dutch oven, brown the raccoon pieces slowly on all sides over medium-high heat. Remove and set it aside.

In the same pot, add onions, carrots, parsnips, sweet potato, beet, and garlic. Cook for 5 minutes.

Add broth, the vinegar, tomato paste, thyme, and bay leaves. Stir well.

Return the raccoon meat to the pot and bring to a simmer. Then, cover the pot and transfer to the preheated oven.

Cook for 3-4 hours, or until the meat is very tender and falling off the bone.

Remove bay leaves before serving.

I had a friend who was raised in the country. Specifically in Alabama. This is a story from her childhood.

She had a little dog she truly loved. (Some of you can see where this is going.)

One day, her dog didn't come home. She searched for it for a whole day. But there was no trace of it. She was heartbroken.

Well, that night the family had a raccoon, or 'coon, for dinner. There it was. Beautifully presented whole in the skillet. Gravy was glistening and veggies were ready.

My friend screamed. She shouted and cried that they cooked her dog. She was inconsolable. The family laughed and soon the dog appeared, after all.

10

Scythe and Seed

Ok, ok, maybe I kinda took you a bit off the beaten path. Here's a wild turkey recipe. But you have to catch them first!

Wild Turkey and Gooseberry Stew

Ingredients you will need:

- 2 lbs wild turkey meat, cubed
- 1 cup fresh or dried gooseberries
- 1 onion, chopped
- 2 carrots, sliced
- 2 celery stalks, chopped (or lovage)
- 2 tbsp cooking oil
- 2 tbsp flour
- 1 tsp dried thyme
- 4 cups chicken broth, turkey broth, or mushroom broth
- Salt and pepper to taste

Instructions:

In a large pot, heat the oil over medium heat. Add the turkey cubes and brown on all sides, about 5-7 minutes. Don't rush.

Remove turkey and set aside. In the same pot, add onions, carrots, and celery. Cook until they are a bit softened, about 5 minutes.

Sprinkle flour over the vegetables and stir to coat. Then cook for 1 minute.

Slowly add chicken broth, stirring constantly to prevent lumps.

Add the browned turkey, the gooseberries thyme, salt, and pepper. Bring to a boil, then reduce heat to low.

Cover and simmer for 1.5 to 2 hours, or until the turkey is tender and the yummy stew has thickened.

You can add and tweak the seasonings as needed before serving. Always taste when you cook.

Serve hot with crusty bread, warm cider, and dehydrated onions.

Sorry, no funny Alabama stories about wild turkeys. However, I do have a great memory of being blockaded by a seemingly half mile long parade of them in the woods. They were so proud.

Have you ever seen a turkey do a threat display dance? They are so fiercely funny. But don't be fooled. They can really hurt you.

If you find yourself hemmed up by a turkey don't try to grab it unless you are experienced. Maybe not then, either. Anyway, you can use an umbrella to feed them off of you. Maybe singing an Adam Sandler song will help.

You can't just eat meat all the time. Vegetables and fruits, greens, and other foods are just as important. So let's turn our attention to them.

Right now the gardens are looking kinda like kale, cabbage, and other brassicas are thriving everywhere. The squash has grown to massive proportions. What will we do if they become sentient? We have to prevent this green takeover by taking out our forks. It's the only way to be sure.

Roasted Butternut Squash Soup

Ingredients you will need:

- 1 large butternut squash, peeled and cubed (don't let it intimidate you)
- 1 onion, diced
- 2 cloves garlic, minced
- 4 cups vegetable broth

13

- 1/2 cup heavy cream
- 2 tbsp olive oil
- Salt and pepper to taste
- 1/4 tsp nutmeg

Instructions:

Preheat your oven to 400°F (200°C).

Coat the butternut squash cubes with 1 tbsp olive oil, salt, and pepper. Spread on a baking sheet, or in a skillet on parchment paper.

Roast for 25-30 minutes, until tender and lightly browned.

(While you wait, read a book, or crochet something cool. Maybe you could listen to a couple of episodes of the My Magical Cottagecore Life podcast.)

In a big pot, sauté onion and garlic in 1 tbsp olive oil over medium heat until softened.

Add roasted squash and vegetable broth. Bring to a boil, then simmer for 15 minutes.

Blend the soup, and syrup if you like, until smooth using an immersion blender or regular blender.

Now stir in the heavy cream and nutmeg. Season with salt and pepper to taste.

Serve hot, garnished with a swirl of cream and a sprinkle of nutmeg.

(Think about roasting the seeds, or saving them for planting.)

So, some of us might like quinoa. Some do not. It's a texture thing. I hear you, Friends. Here's a rice recipe.

Butternut Squash and Sage Risotto

Ingredients you will need:

- 1 1/2 cups Arborio rice (fancy tonight)
- 4 cups vegetable broth, kept warm
- 1 cup butternut squash, diced small
- 1/2 cup white wine
- 1 onion, finely diced
- 2 cloves garlic, minced
- 2 tbsp olive oil
- 2 tbsp butter
- 1/4 cup grated Parmesan cheese
- 2 tbsp fresh sage, chopped
- Salt and pepper to taste

Instructions:

In a soup pot, heat olive oil over medium heat.

Add onion and garlic, sauté until softened. Sweat them.

Then add butternut squash and cook for 5 minutes.

Add the rice and stir to coat with oil. Toast for 1-2 minutes.

Pour in white wine and stir until absorbed.

Begin adding warm broth, 1/2 cup at a time, stirring constantly and waiting for each addition to be absorbed before adding more.

Continue this process until your rice is creamy and al dente, about 18-20 minutes.

Stir in butter, Parmesan, and sage. You can season with salt and pepper.

Eat it while it's hot.

Despite the fervor for all things pumpkin spice in autumn, some people love apples just as much. Adding them to savory dishes helps use up all those apples in the yard. It also can get people to try things that are new. Especially stroller citizens (children).

The purple topped turnips are really cool to watch shrivel up into brown husks. This can be accomplished by ignoring their presence in the pantry until they are forgotten.

Apple and Swede (Turnip) Gratin

Ingredients you will need:

- 2 large purple top turnips, thinly sliced
- 2 large apples, thinly sliced
- 1 cup heavy cream
- 1 cup grated Gruyère cheese
- 2 tbsp fresh thyme leaves
- Salt and white pepper to taste
- 2 tbsp butter

Instructions:

Preheat your oven to 375°F (190°C).

Grease a 9x13 inch baking dish with butter.

Now, layer out the turnip and apple slices alternately in the dish. Make it pretty. We eat with our eyes, too.

In a bowl, mix the heavy cream, 3/4 cup of the cheese, thyme, salt, and white pepper. Pour it over the turnips and apples.

Cover with foil, or 2 layers parchment paper, and bake for 30 minutes.

Remove the foil, sprinkle remaining cheese on top, and bake for another 15-20 minutes until it's all bubbly and golden.

Let cool for 10 minutes before serving.

Roasted Sweet Potato, Pumpkin Seeds, and Black Bean Tacos

Ingredients you will need:

- 2 large sweet potatoes, peeled and diced
- 1 can (15 oz) black beans, drained and rinsed
- 1 red onion, sliced
- 2 tbsp olive oil
- 1 tsp ground cumin
- 1 tsp smoked paprika
- Salt and pepper to taste
- 8 small corn tortillas
- 1 avocado, sliced
- 1/4 cup chopped cilantro
- crushed, shelled, salted pumpkin seeds
- Lime wedges for serving

Instructions:

Preheat the oven to 425°F (220°C).

Toss sweet potatoes and red onion with olive oil, cumin, smoked paprika, salt, and pepper.

Spread on a baking sheet and roast for 25-30 minutes, stirring halfway through.

Warm black beans in a small skillet.

Heat tortillas according to package instructions.

Assemble your tacos:

Fill each tortilla with roasted sweet potatoes, black beans, and sliced avocado.

19

Garnish with crushed pumpkin seeds, cilantro and serve with lime wedges.

Did you know a sweet potato is not an actual yam? We talked about this on the show. All my early life, I referred to them as yams. Oooooh, the disrespect.
19
You can eat their leaves, too. In fact, you could stuff them with this hash. That all depends on the time of year, though.

Kale and Sweet Potato Hash

Ingredients you will need:

- 2 large sweet potatoes, diced
- 1 bunch kale, stems removed and chopped
- 1 onion, diced
- 2 cloves garlic, minced

- 2 tbsp olive oil, or vegetable shortening
- 1 tsp smoked paprika
- Salt and pepper to taste (optional)

Instructions:

Heat olive oil, or vegetable shortening, in a large skillet over medium heat.

Add sweet potatoes and onion. Cook for 10-12 minutes, stirring occasionally. Reduce heat, if needed. You do not want this to burn.

Add the garlic and smoked paprika to taste, and cook for another minute. Add the kale and cook until wilted, like my dreams of world cheese domination, about 5 minutes.

Roasted Beet and Goat Cheese Salad

Ingredients you will need:

- 4 medium beets, peeled and cut into wedges
- 6 cups mixed salad greens
- 4 oz goat cheese, crumbled
- 1/4 cup chopped walnuts, toasted
- 2 tbsp olive oil
- 2 tbsp balsamic vinegar
- 1 tbsp honey
- Salt and pepper to taste

Instructions:

Preheat the oven to 400°F (200°C).

Toss beet wedges with 1 tbsp olive oil, salt, and pepper.

Roast on a baking sheet for 25-30 minutes until tender.

In a small bowl, whisk together remaining olive oil, balsamic vinegar, and honey.

In a large salad bowl, toss salad greens with half of the dressing.

Arrange the greens on plates and top with roasted beets, crumbled goat cheese, and walnuts.

Drizzle with remaining dressing and serve quickly.

Stuffed Acorn Squash with Quinoa and Cranberries

Ingredients you will need:

- 2 acorn squashes, halved and seeded
- 1 cup quinoa
- 2 cups vegetable broth
- 1/2 cup dried cranberries
- 1/4 cup chopped pecans
- 2 tbsp olive oil
- 1 tsp dried sage
- Salt and pepper to taste

Instructions:

Preheat the oven to 400°F (200°C).

Brush squash halves with 1 tbsp olive oil, season with salt and pepper.

Place the cut-side down on a baking sheet and roast them until tender. Usually this takes about 30 minutes.

Meanwhile, rinse the quinoa and cook in vegetable broth according to package instructions.
Then mix the cooked quinoa with cranberries, pecans, any remaining olive oil, and sage.

Flip squash halves over and fill with quinoa mixture. Then return to the oven for 10 minutes to heat through.

Parsnip and Apple Soup

Ingredients you will need:

- 4 large parsnips, peeled and chopped
- 2 apples, peeled and chopped
- 1 onion, diced
- 3 cloves garlic, minced
- 4 cups vegetable broth
- 1/2 cup heavy cream
- 2 tbsp butter
- 1 tsp ground coriander
- ½ tsp allspice or powdered spicebush
- Salt and white pepper to taste

Instructions:

Melt butter in a Dutch oven or big pot over medium heat.
Add onion and garlic (the allium dream team), sauté until softened.

Add the parsnips, apples, and coriander. Cook for 5 minutes.

Pour in the vegetable broth, bring to a boil, then simmer for 20 minutes
until the vegetables are tender.
Blend the soup until smooth.

Stir in the heavy cream, and season with salt and pepper.

Simmer for an additional 5 minutes, then serve.

Roasted Brussels Sprouts, for Children Who Dislike Them, with a Balsamic Glaze

Ingredients you will need:

- 1 lb Brussels sprouts, trimmed and halved
- 2 tbsp olive oil
- 1/4 cup balsamic vinegar
- 2 tbsp orange thyme honey (regular is fine, though)
- Salt and pepper to taste

Instructions:

Preheat the oven to 425°F (220°C).

Coat Brussel sprouts with olive oil, salt, and pepper.

Spread on a baking sheet and roast for 20-25 minutes, shimmying the baking sheet halfway through.

Meanwhile, in a small pan, combine the balsamic vinegar and honey.

Simmer over medium heat until reduced by half and thickened

Drizzle the glaze over the roasted Brussels sprouts.

Toss to coat and serve immediately. This is great to partner with dressing or stuffing. THEY ARE NOT THE SAME THING.

Roasted Brussels Sprouts with Cranberries and Pecans

Ingredients you will need:

- 1 lb Brussels sprouts, trimmed and halved
- 1/2 cup fresh cranberries
- 1/3 cup chopped pecans
- 2 tbsp olive oil
- 2 tbsp maple syrup
- 1 tbsp balsamic vinegar
- Salt and pepper to taste

Instructions:

Preheat the oven to 400°F (200°C).

In a large bowl, toss Brussels sprouts with olive oil, salt, and pepper.

Spread on a baking sheet and roast for 20 minutes.

In a small bowl, mix maple syrup and balsamic vinegar.

Add cranberries and pecans to the baking sheet, drizzle with maple mixture.

Toss to coat and roast for an additional 5-10 minutes until Brussels sprouts are caramelized and cranberries are soft.

Serve them hot, as a side dish.

Maple Crabapple Glazed Root Vegetables

Ingredients you will:

- 2 carrots, peeled and cut into chunks
- 2 parsnips, peeled and cut into chunks
- 1 large sweet potato, peeled and cut into chunks
- 1 red onion, cut into wedges
- 1/4 cup maple syrup
- 2 tbsp olive oil
- 1 tbsp fresh rosemary, chopped
- ¼ cup dehydrated crabapples, chopped
- Salt and pepper to taste

Instructions:

Preheat the oven to 400°F (200°C).

In a large bowl, toss all the vegetables and crabapples with olive oil, salt, and pepper.

Spread on a baking sheet and roast for 25 minutes.

In a small bowl, mix maple syrup and rosemary. Drizzle over the vegetables and crabapples, and toss to coat.

Return to the oven for another 10-15 minutes, until vegetables are tender and caramelized.

This is good to eat when you have a stomach cold and don't want meat.

Roasted Acorn Squash Soup with Sage Croutons

Ingredients you will need:

- 2 acorn squashes, halved and seeded
- 1 onion, diced
- 2 cloves garlic, minced
- 4 cups vegetable broth, turkey broth, or goat broth
- 1/2 cup heavy cream
- 2 tbsp olive oil
- 1 tsp dried sage
- Salt and pepper to taste
- For croutons:
  - 2 cups cubed day-old bread
  - 2 tbsp olive oil
  - 1 tbsp fresh sage, finely chopped
  - Salt to taste

Instructions:

Preheat the oven to 400°F (200°C).

Brush squash halves with 1 tbsp olive oil, season with salt and pepper.

Roast cut-side down for 35-40 minutes until tender.

In a rather large pot, sauté onion and garlic in 1 tbsp olive oil until softened.

Scoop out roasted squash and add to the pot with vegetable broth and dried sage.

Simmer for 15 minutes, then blend until smooth.

Stir in heavy cream and season with salt and pepper.

For croutons:

Toss bread cubes with olive oil, fresh sage, and salt. Bake at 375°F (190°C) for 10-12 minutes until golden.

Serve soup hot, topped with sage croutons.

You know, you don't have to just stop at sage croutons. You can make delicious sage butter. Using regular green sage is tasty. But you can experiment with purple sage, or even pineapple sage.

Or, if you have a sweeter tooth, you can make sage infused honeys. We talked about how easy these are to make. Slathering some over freshly baked rolls are a great side to this soup.

Let's keep the veggie train going! Chugga chugga toot toot! We need fortifying vitamins to prepare for the cold.

Caramelized Onion and Apple Tart

Ingredients you will need:

- 1 sheet puff pastry, thawed
- 3 large onions, thinly sliced
- 2 apples, thinly sliced
- 2 tbsp butter
- 1 tbsp olive oil
- 1 tbsp fresh thyme leaves
- 1/4 cup crumbled blue cheese
- 2 tbsp balsamic vinegar
- Salt and pepper to taste

Instructions:

Preheat the oven to 400°F (200°C).

In a large skillet (cuz you need room for this one) melt butter with olive oil over medium heat.

Add the onions and cook, stirring occasionally, for 25-30 minutes until caramelized.

Stir in balsamic vinegar and cook for 2 more minutes. Set aside to cool slightly.

Roll out puff pastry on a baking sheet lined with parchment paper.

Spread your caramelized onions over the pastry, leaving a 1-inch border.

Arrange the apple slices on top and sprinkle with thyme, salt, and pepper.

Fold over the edges of the pastry to create a border.
Bake for 20-25 minutes until the pastry is golden brown. Depending on your oven, you may have reduced temp to avoid burning.

Sprinkle blue cheese over the tart and bake for an additional 5 minutes.

 Serve warm, cut into squares.

Time for some more green vegetables. Specifically it's time for some leafy greens. My parents who raised me were from the South. My parents who didn't raise me were raised by people from the South. Therefore, if I don't include one recipe with collard greens I think I'll be ejected from the Diaspora. My speckled roasting pan may vanish.

While we're on the topic of growing things and where they grow, let's talk about quinoa. Eating it doesn't make you better or worse than anyone else. Just remember, that there are ways that we can eat things from far away without having to be weird about it.

If you serve it, keep in mind that somebody might not want to try it. And that's okay. They can eat other parts of the meal.

Stuffed Collard Greens, Lamb's Quarter, Quinoa and Black Beans

Ingredients you will need:

- 8 large collard green leaves
- 1 cup cooked quinoa
- ¼ cup minced Lamb's Quarter
- 1 can (15 oz) black beans, drained and rinsed
- 1 red bell pepper, diced
- 1/4 cup chopped cilantro
- 2 tbsp olive oil
- 1 tbsp lime juice
- 1 tsp ground cumin
- Salt and pepper to taste
- 1 cup tomato sauce

Instructions:

Preheat the oven to 375°F (190°C).

Blanch collard leaves in boiling water for 2 minutes, then shock in ice water. Pat dry.

In a bowl, mix quinoa, Lamb's Quarter, black beans, bell pepper, cilantro, 1 tbsp olive oil, lime juice, cumin, salt, and pepper.

Place a portion of the mixture in the center of each collard leaf and roll up, tucking in the sides.

Arrange rolls seam-side down in a baking dish, the. Pour tomato sauce over the rolls and drizzle with remaining olive oil.

Cover with foil and bake for 25-30 minutes until heated through.

Serve hot, or take to potluck wrapped in foil, garnished with additional cilantro if desired.

I'm one of those people who cook with cilantro but still think it tastes like soap. I've grown accustomed to its taste.

So I am here to tell you it's ok to substitute parsley if you are like me and cooking for just yourself.

My family likes cilantro.

Sigh.

If you're a long time listener of the show, you already know that my husband fishes. Like, fishes a lot. He's in a fishing club. We go to fishing conventions.

So if I didn't put a fish recipe in this book, I don't know if I'd still be able to look my husband in the eyes. But since I like sweet meats and he doesn't, this is where I get to put a sweet recipe.

Maple-Glazed Salmon with Autumn Berry Compote

Ingredients you will need:

For the salmon:

- 4 salmon filets (app. 6 oz each)
- 1/4 cup maple syrup
- 2 tbsp soy sauce
- 1 tbsp Dijon mustard
- 1 clove garlic, minced
- Salt and pepper to taste

For the berry compote:

- 2 cups mixed berries (blackberries, raspberries, and/or blueberries)
- 1/4 cup apple cider
- 2 tbsp honey
- 1 cinnamon stick
- 1 star anise (optional, if you don't like black licorice)
- Zest of 1 orange

For the garnish:

- 1/4 cup toasted pumpkin seeds

Instructions:

Preheat the oven to 400°F (200°C).

In a small bowl, whisk together maple syrup, soy sauce, Dijon mustard, and minced garlic.

Place salmon filets in a baking dish and season with salt and pepper. Pour the maple mixture over the salmon, ensuring it's well coated.

Bake the salmon for 12-15 minutes, or until it flakes easily with a fork.

While the salmon is baking, prepare the berry compote. In a saucepan, combine berries, apple cider, honey, cinnamon stick, star anise, and orange zest.

Bring the mixture to a simmer over medium heat. Cook for about 10 minutes, stirring occasionally, until the berries have broken down and the sauce has thickened slightly.

Remove the cinnamon stick and star anise from the compote. Toast the pumpkin seeds in a dry skillet over medium heat for 3-5 minutes, stirring frequently until golden.

Serve the baked salmon topped with a generous spoonful of the warm berry compote and a sprinkle of toasted pumpkin seeds.

Michigan Smoked Chub with Cedar, Nuts, and Fall Fruits (No Maple Syrup)

Ingredients you will need:

- 2 smoked chub filets (about 8 oz each)
- 1 cedar plank, soaked in water for at least 1 hour
- 1/2 cup mixed nuts (walnuts, pecans, and hazelnuts), roughly chopped
- 1 cup mixed fall fruits (apples, pears, and dried cranberries), diced
- 2 tbsp olive oil, divided
- 1 tbsp fresh thyme leaves
- 1 tsp orange zest
- 1 tbsp fresh orange juice
- 1 tsp honey (optional)
- Salt and freshly ground black pepper to taste
- Lemon wedges for serving

Instructions:

Preheat your grill to medium-high heat about 375°F to 400°F (190°C to 200°C).

In a bowl, mix the diced fall fruits with 1 tbsp of olive oil, orange zest, orange juice, and honey (if using). Add a pinch of salt and set aside.

In another bowl, toss the chopped nuts with 1/2 tbsp of olive oil, 1 tsp of fresh thyme leaves, and a pinch of salt and pepper.

Place the soaked cedar plank on the preheated grill and close the lid. Heat for about 3-5 minutes or until the plank begins to smoke and crackle.

Carefully flip the plank and place the smoked chub filets on top, skin-side down.

Brush the chub with the remaining 1/2 tbsp of olive oil and sprinkle with black pepper and the remaining thyme leaves.

Close the grill lid and cook for about 10-12 minutes, or until the fish is heated through and the edges are lightly caramelized.

In the last 2-3 minutes of cooking, sprinkle the nut mixture over the fish and around the plank. Close the lid to let the nuts toast slightly.

Remove the plank from the grill carefully using heat-resistant gloves or tongs.

Spoon the fruit mix around the fish on the plank.

Serve immediately on the cedar plank, with lemon wedges on the side.

Michigan Smoked Chub with Cedar, Nuts, and Fall Fruits WITH Maple Syrup

Ingredients:

- 2 smoked chub filets (about 8 oz each)
- 1 cedar plank, soaked in water for at least 1 hour
- 1/2 cup mixed nuts (walnuts, pecans, and hazelnuts), roughly chopped
- 1 cup mixed fall fruits (apples, pears, and cranberries), diced
- 2 tbsp maple syrup
- 1 tbsp olive oil
- 1 tsp fresh thyme leaves
- Salt and freshly ground black pepper to taste
- Lemon wedges for serving

Instructions:

Preheat your grill to medium-high heat about 375°F to 400°F (190°C to 200°C).

In a non metal bowl, mix the diced fall fruits with 1 tbsp of maple syrup and a pinch of salt. Set aside.

In another bowl, toss the chopped nuts with 1 tbsp of olive oil, 1 tsp of fresh thyme leaves, and a pinch of salt and pepper.

Place the soaked cedar plank on the preheated grill and close the lid. Heat for about 3-5 minutes or until the plank begins to smoke and crackle.

Carefully flip the plank and place the smoked chub filets on top, skin-side down.

Brush the chub with the remaining 1 tbsp of maple syrup and sprinkle with a little black pepper.

Close the grill lid and cook for about 10-12 minutes, or until the fish is heated through and the edges are lightly caramelized.

In the last 2-3 minutes of cooking, sprinkle the nut mixture over the fish and around the plank. Close the lid to let the nuts toast slightly.

Remove the plank from the grill carefully using heat-resistant gloves or tongs.

Spoon the fruit mix around the fish on the plank.

Serve immediately on the cedar plank, with lemon wedges on the side.

Michigan Whitefish with Cantaloupe and Fall Seeds

Ingredients you will need:

- 4 Michigan whitefish filets (6-8 oz each)
- 1 medium cantaloupe, diced
- 1/4 cup pumpkin seeds
- 2 tbsp sunflower seeds
- 2 tbsp olive oil
- 2 tbsp fresh lemon juice
- 1 tbsp fresh thyme leaves
- 1 tsp ground coriander
- Salt and freshly ground black pepper to taste
- 2 tbsp butter
- Fresh parsley for garnish

Instructions:

Preheat the oven to 400°F (200°C).

In a bowl, combine the diced cantaloupe, pumpkin seeds, and sunflower seeds. Set aside.

In a small bowl, whisk together 1 tbsp olive oil, lemon juice, thyme, and coriander. Season with salt and pepper.

Pat the whitefish filets dry with paper towels. Season both sides with salt and pepper.

Heat the remaining 1 tbsp olive oil in a large oven-safe skillet over medium-high heat.
39

Once hot, add the whitefish filets skin-side down. Cook for 3-4 minutes until the skin is crispy.

Flip the filets and transfer the skillet to the preheated oven. Bake for 5-7 minutes, or until the fish is cooked through and flakes easily.

While the fish is in the oven, melt the butter in a separate pan over medium heat. Add the cantaloupe and seed mixture, cooking for 2-3 minutes until the cantaloupe is slightly softened and the seeds are toasted.

Remove the fish from the oven. Plate each filet and top with the warm cantaloupe and seed mixture.

Drizzle the herb and lemon dressing over each filet.

Garnish with fresh parsley and serve immediately.

If Michigan whitefish is unavailable, you can substitute with another mild, white fish like halibut or cod. It's fine. The texture will be a little different, that's all.

.

I grew up eating chub, sable, panfish, catfish, bass, and etc. I don't eat all fish now, but I still love a good smoked fish. My Mama used to work at Ma Cohen's. But back then, it was called Sea Fare Foods. I still love their pickled herring in a jar.

Are you hiding again? The children complained about eating so many greens earlier? Grab a cup of tea, or a glass of bubbly grape juice, and eat this while they wash the dishes.

Pear and Ginger Crisp

Ingredients you will need:

- 6 ripe pears, peeled, cored, and sliced
- 1/4 cup granulated sugar
- 1 tbsp lemon juice
- 1 tbsp fresh ginger, grated
- 1 tsp ground cinnamon
- For topping:
  - 1 cup rolled oats
  - 1/2 cup all-purpose flour
  - 1/2 cup brown sugar
  - 1/2 cup cold butter, cubed
  - 1/4 cup chopped pecans
  - 1/4 tsp salt

Instructions:

Preheat the oven to 350°F (175°C).

In a large bowl, gently mix pears with sugar, lemon juice, ginger, and cinnamon. Then transfer to a 9x13 inch baking dish.

For topping:

In a bowl, mix oats, flour, brown sugar, and salt.

Cut in cold butter until mixture is crumbly.

Stir in chopped pecans and sprinkle topping evenly over the pears.

Bake for 40-45 minutes until topping is golden and filling is bubbly.

Let cool for 15 minutes before serving.

Serve warm with vanilla ice cream if desired. Eat in the closet if you're hiding from your children.

Just know, they will find you. They can smell goodies. So eat fast.

But you do have a way to stave them off if you're not adverse to baking in advance. Those pumpkins are just waiting for you to save them from turning into Jack-o'-lanterns.

It's kinda a semi fact that children are somehow magnetically drawn to pumpkin bread. So it could buy you some time. Just bake it and leave it on the counter.

How about a double team with some movies produced by a huge studio with a big eared mascot? I'm not mentioning them by name. The Mouse Knows and will come for you.

Spiced Pumpkin Bread

Ingredients you will need:

- 1 3/4 cups all-purpose flour
- 1 cup pumpkin puree
- 1 cup granulated sugar
- 1/2 cup vegetable oil
- 2 eggs
- 1 tsp baking soda
- 1/2 tsp baking powder
- 1/2 tsp salt
- 1 tsp ground cinnamon
- 1/2 tsp ground nutmeg
- 1/4 tsp ground cloves
- 1/4 cup water

Instructions:

Preheat the oven to 350°F (175°C). Grease a 9x5 inch loaf pan.

In a really big bowl, mix pumpkin puree, sugar, oil, and eggs until well blended.

In another bowl, whisk together flour, baking soda, baking powder, salt, and spices.

Gradually stir the dry ingredients into the pumpkin mixture, alternating with water.

Pour batter into the prepared loaf pan.

Bake for 60-65 minutes, or until a toothpick inserted in the center comes out clean. Know your oven. Adjust temperature as needed.

Cool in the pan for 10 minutes, then remove and cool completely on a wire rack.

Slice and leave out the cake plate while you hide in the closet.

This is also a great time to make dehydrated apple slices. They really are a good healthy snack for children and non-children to eat. They're good for you. Well, at least if you're not allergic to apples.

They also help you use up those apples that are all over the place that are falling from the trees right now if it's fall where you are. And yes, in the United States we really do call Autumn Fall.

You could go the extra mile and make a batch of spiced cider. Adding dark cherries makes this really rich. The rose petals are for style and a light taste.

Spiced Apple Cider

Ingredients you will need:

- 8 cups apple cider
- 2 cinnamon sticks
- 1 orange, sliced
- 4 whole cloves
- ⅓ cup rose water
- 1 cup rose petals
- ½ cup chopped, pitted dark cherries
- 2 star anise
- 1/4 cup brown sugar (optional)

Instructions:

In a large pot, combine all the ingredients and bring to a simmer over medium heat.

Reduce heat to low and let simmer for 15-20 minutes.

Strain out the spices and orange slices.

Serve hot, garnished with a cinnamon stick and orange slice if desired

Ummm, you can add some rum to this. It will make it for adults who like that kind of thing. You can brandy. You can add cognac.
You can add whiskey.

WAIT, NOT ALL AT THE SAME TIME!

You know what? Let's make some things everyone can enjoy together. These are easy, so we can just make them and not go back to hide with our secret ice cream stash.

Cinnamon Apple and Pumpkin Seed Parfait

Ingredients you will need:

- 2 apples, diced
- 1 tsp cinnamon
- 2 cups Greek yogurt
- 1/4 cup pumpkin seeds
- 2 tbsp honey

Instructions:

Toast pumpkin seeds in a dry skillet over medium heat for 3-5 minutes, stirring frequently until golden. Set aside to cool.

Toss diced apples with cinnamon in a bowl.

In glasses, layer: 1/4 cup yogurt, 1/4 of the apple mixture, and 1 tbsp toasted pumpkin seeds. Repeat layers.

Drizzle each parfait with 1/2 tbsp honey and sprinkle with extra cinnamon.

Pear and Sunflower Seed Salad

Ingredients you will need:

- 2 ripe pears, thinly sliced
- 4 cups baby spinach
- 1/4 cup sunflower seeds
- 1/4 cup crumbled blue cheese
- 2 tbsp balsamic vinegar
- 2 tbsp olive oil
- Salt and pepper to taste

Instructions:

Toast the sunflower seeds in a dry skillet over medium heat for 2-3 minutes, stirring frequently until golden. Set aside to cool.

Whisk together balsamic vinegar and olive oil in a small bowl. Season with salt and pepper.

In a large salad bowl, toss spinach with half the dressing.

Add sliced pears, toasted sunflower seeds, and blue cheese.

Drizzle remaining dressing over the salad and toss gently to combine.

Dried Squash and Cranberry Granola Bars

Ingredients you will need:

- 2 cups rolled oats
- 1/2 cup dried cranberries
- 1/2 cup dried squash pieces
- 1/2 cup chopped nuts (almonds or walnuts)
- 1/3 cup honey
- 1/4 cup unsalted butter
- 1/4 cup brown sugar
- 1 tsp vanilla extract
- 1/4 tsp salt

Instructions:

Preheat the oven to 350°F (175°C). Line an 8-inch square baking pan with parchment paper.

In a large bowl, mix oats, dried cranberries, dried squash, and chopped nuts.

In a small saucepan, combine honey, butter, and brown sugar. Heat over medium heat, stirring until butter is melted and mixture is smooth.

Remove from heat and stir in vanilla extract and salt.
Pour the honey mixture over the oat mixture and stir until well combined.

Press the mixture firmly into the prepared baking pan.

Bake for 25-30 minutes, until golden brown at the edges.

Allow to cool completely in the pan before cutting into bars.

I

have to say, we need to add something unexpected. This next recipe is good for the tweens and teens. Getting them into the kitchen is always good for their future.

PLUS it will get them to give figs a chance. Some children have a hesitant reaction to trying them. A great way to fix this is to have them cook them!

Roasted Pumpkin Seed and Fig Compote

Ingredients you will need:

- 1 lb fresh figs, chopped
- 1/4 cup orange juice
- 2 tbsp honey
- 1 cinnamon stick
- 1/4 cup pumpkin seeds
- Pinch of salt

Instructions:

In a medium saucepan, combine chopped figs, orange juice, honey, and cinnamon stick. Bring to a simmer over medium heat.

Reduce heat to low and cook, stirring occasionally, for 15-20 minutes until figs are soft and mixture has thickened.

While the compote is cooking, toast pumpkin seeds in a dry skillet over medium heat for 3-5 minutes, stirring frequently until golden. Set aside to cool.

Remove cinnamon stick from the compote and stir in a pinch of salt. Let the compote cool for 5 minutes, then stir in the toasted pumpkin seeds.

Serve warm or at room temperature over Greek yogurt or oatmeal.

Did you know you can substitute roasted squash seeds for roasted pumpkin seeds?

That's right. You don't have to throw out those acorn squash seeds, those Hubbard squash seeds, or etc. You can save them and roast them. It's good for you. They taste good.

Although I do realize some of you cannot eat squash, I strongly recommend that those who do not have an allergy should try it. You may find that making your own at home is a lot more cost efficient than buying them at the grocery store or the gas station. And when you make your own food products, or process your own food products, you know exactly what went in them.

Another good thing about making something like this at home, it teaches you patience and mindfulness. We could all use a little bit more mindfulness.

Being present in the moment also helps people not get into misunderstandings.

You begin to be able to hear each other.

Now?

What was I saying?

Oh yeah.

Truly listening avoids drama.

Truly listening to the My Magical Cottagecore Life podcast avoids boredom.

And on that note, here's a bread

No Drama Banana Blueberry Bread

Ingredients you will need:

- 1/2 cup chopped walnuts
- 2 cups all purpose flour
- 1 tbsp baking powder
- 1 tsp salt
- 1 1/4 c milk of any kind
- 3 overripe medium bananas, mashed
- 1 handful of frozen blueberries (about 20)
- Butter or spray oil

Preheat the oven at 325° F (162°C).

In a large bowl mix dry ingredients.

Mix dry ingredients and banana mush together by hand.

Add milk, a 1/4 cup at a time.

Mix by hand or spatula. Then fold in the blueberries.
Do not over mix.

Add to the buttered, or sprayed, loaf pan. Or use margarine in a loaf
pan, and parchment paper, I'm not the boss of you.

Bake for about 30 minutes OR until a bamboo skewer comes out clean.
Don't over cook. Loaf will not be overly sweet.

Now you know I'm from Michigan , Y'all. There's no way I can let you go without a couple of more special recipes dedicated to the people from the land of the freshwater seas.

Venison Medallions with Date and Pomegranate Sauce

Ingredients you will need:

- 1 lb venison loin, cut into 1-inch thick medallions
- Salt and freshly ground black pepper
- 2 tbsp olive oil
- 1/2 cup red wine
- 1/4 cup balsamic vinegar
- 1/2 cup pitted and chopped dates
- 1/2 cup pomegranate seeds
- 1/4 cup pomegranate juice
- 2 tbsp butter
- Fresh thyme for garnish

Instructions:

Remove the venison from the refrigerator 30 minutes before cooking. Season generously with salt and pepper.

Preheat the oven to 375°F (190°C).

Heat olive oil in a large oven-safe skillet over high heat. When the oil is shimmering, add the venison medallions and sear for 2-3 minutes on each side until browned.

Transfer the skillet to the preheated oven and cook for 5-7 minutes for medium-rare (internal temperature of 130-135°F or 54-57°C). Remove from the oven and transfer the venison to a plate. Tent with foil to rest.

5. Return the skillet to the stovetop over medium heat. Add red wine and balsamic vinegar, scraping up any browned bits from the bottom of the pan.

6. Add chopped dates, pomegranate seeds, and pomegranate juice. Simmer for 5-7 minutes until the sauce has reduced and thickened slightly.

7. Remove from heat and stir in butter until melted and incorporated.

8. Slice the venison medallions against the grain and arrange on plates. Spoon the warm date and pomegranate sauce over the venison.

9. Garnish with fresh thyme and additional pomegranate seeds if desired.

Serve immediately, perhaps with roasted root vegetables or a wild rice pilaf for a complete fall-inspired meal.

Autumn Harvest Chicken with Acorn-Blueberry Sauce

Ingredients you will need:

- 4 boneless, skinless chicken breasts
- Salt and freshly ground black pepper
- 2 tbsp olive oil
- 1/2 cup acorn flour (ground from leached acorns)
- 1 cup fresh blueberries
- 1/4 cup maple syrup
- 1/4 cup apple cider vinegar
- 1 tbsp fresh thyme leaves
- 2 cloves garlic, minced
- 1 small butternut squash, peeled and cubed
- 2 medium parsnips, peeled and cut into sticks
- 1 large red onion, cut into wedges
- 2 tbsp butter

Instructions:

Preheat the oven to 400°F (200°C).

In a shallow dish, mix the acorn flour with 1 tsp salt and 1/2 tsp black pepper. Dredge the chicken breasts in this mixture, shaking off excess.

Heat your olive oil in a large oven-safe skillet over medium-high heat. Add the chicken breasts and cook for 3-4 minutes on each side until golden brown. Transfer the skillet to the preheated oven and cook for 15-20 minutes, or until the internal temperature of the chicken reaches 165°F (74°C).

While the chicken is cooking, prepare the vegetables. Toss the butternut squash, parsnips, and red onion with 1 tbsp olive oil, salt, and pepper. Spread on a baking sheet and roast in the oven alongside the chicken for about 25-30 minutes, stirring once halfway through.

5. For the sauce, combine blueberries, maple syrup, apple cider vinegar, thyme, and garlic in a small saucepan. Bring to a simmer over medium

heat and cook for about 10 minutes, stirring occasionally, until the blueberries have burst and the sauce has thickened slightly.

6. Once the chicken is done, remove it from the oven and let it rest for 5 minutes. In the same skillet, melt the butter and add any juices from the resting chicken to the blueberry sauce, stirring to combine.

7. Serve the chicken breasts on a bed of roasted fall vegetables, topped with the acorn-blueberry sauce.

I love sharing things with my friends, and we're friends, right?

I also look forward to sharing some time with you on the podcast and in the social media groups. Small places can hold big feelings.

So til next time I take up my pen, I will meet you in the airways on the My Magical Cottagecore Life Podcast on Spotify, and other platforms.

Notes and Tweaks

Scythe and Seed